1,003 Great Things
About Being a Woman

1,003
Great Things About Being
a Woman

Lisa Birnbach, Ann Hodgman, Patricia Marx

**Andrews McMeel
Publishing**

Kansas City

1,003 Great Things About Being a Woman

05 06 07 08 09 TNS 10 9 8 7 6 5 4 3 2 1

ISBN: 0-7407-5013-5

Library of Congress Control Number: 2004111314

Printed in Canada

—— ATTENTION: SCHOOLS AND BUSINESSES ——
Andrews McMeel books are available at quantity discounts with bulk purchase for educational, business, or sales promotional use. For information, please write to: Special Sales Department, Andrews McMeel Publishing, 4520 Main Street, Kansas City, Missouri 64111.

1,003 Great Things
About Being a Woman

You and the children
go first in the lifeboat.

❁

Women are so much
better at gossip than men.

When's the last time you
met a man brave enough to
ask directions?

Without women, where
would the diet industry be?

She's called "*Lady Liberty.*"

Two X chromosomes!

No prostate problems!

Separate stalls for peeing.

They don't call us the
fairer sex for nothing.

Hair talk is the
international language.

All that time saved by not having
to shave your face.

"Sure, God created man before
woman, but then you always make
a rough draft before the final
masterpiece."   —Anonymous

Who would be more fun to shop
with—a hunter or a gatherer?

Want to get out of gym class?
Pretend you have your period.

Why do they like trucks so much?

"The idea of strictly minding our
own business is moldy rubbish.
Who could be so selfish?"
—Myrtie Barker

A new lipstick is guaranteed to
bring an hour of bliss.

No matter how old we are,
we still enjoy reading
wedding announcements.

They tip their hats to us.

"In my sex fantasy, nobody ever
loves me for my mind."
—Nora Ephron

Mother's Day was invented
before Father's Day.

❀

We learn new crafts at the
drop of a (hand-woven) hat.

❀

No more hauling buckets
of water from the well.

❀

Men who wear shoe lifts are dorks,
but women who wear high heels
are glamorously eye-catching.

A woman is so tolerant that in a pinch, she will treat a pint of ice cream as her best friend.

You can never go wrong with gingham.

Without These Women . . .

Without Jackie Kennedy, the
White House might be furnished
today with bean bag chairs.

Without Betty Crocker,
we'd never have gotten
out of the kitchen.

Without Mrs. Claus, Santa would be tinkering in his workshop until February.

(6)

Without Susan B. Anthony, the Susan B. Anthony coin would be blank.

(6)

Without Helen of Troy, Brad Pitt would have been out a movie role.

Without Katharine Hepburn,
Spencer Tracy might have had to
play opposite Margaret Dumont.

⑥

Without Olive Oyl, Popeye wouldn't
have eaten his spinach.

⑥

Without Jack Sprat's wife,
Jack Sprat couldn't have
licked the platter clean.

Without Betsy Ross, the U.S.
flag might feature a baseball.

(6)

Without Beatrice, Dante
wouldn't have given us hell.

(6)

Without Shirley Temple, we
wouldn't have had so many
annoying child actors.

Without Aileen Wurnos, Charlize Theron wouldn't have gotten an Academy Award.

⟲

Without Juliette Low, there wouldn't be Girl Scout cookies.

⟲

Without Eve, Adam would have a rib to spare.

⟲

Without Dolly Madison, ice cream wouldn't be so presidential.

Without Nancy Reagan—
who knows?

⑥

Without Ella Fitzgerald, "A Tisket,
a Tasket" would be just an old-
fashioned children's rhyme.

⑥

Without Jocelyn Wildenstein, we
wouldn't understand the concept
of too much plastic surgery.

Without Tina Turner, a
woman would feel compelled
to dress her age.

⟲

Without Juliet, Romeo might
have hooked up with someone
his parents liked.

⟲

Without Margaret Sanger, one of
our fourteen sisters might have
been writing this book.

Valentine's Day is a big deal to us.

We do understand about money;
we've just decided to play along
and act stupid about it.

Foreign languages come
easier to us.

We can see the light at the end of
a warehouse-sale tunnel.

Women are less squeamish than men. Proof: dirty diapers.

Women are tougher than men. Proof: bikini waxes.

It's *expected* that we sing along with love songs on the radio.

"There is a woman at the beginning of all great things."
—Lamartine

Research indicates that babies
prefer women's voices to men's.

Tinted contact lenses look
ridiculous on guys.

So do manicures.

And don't get us started on
pedicures for men!

"A man has to be Joe McCarthy
to be called ruthless. All a woman
has to do is put you on hold."
—Marlo Thomas

Say what you want—men
look dopey prancing around
in aerobics classes.

You don't have to jump as high
to break the women's high-jump
record as you do for the men's.

"I don't want to get to the end
of my life and find that I lived
just the length of it. I want to
have lived the width of it as well."
—Diane Ackerman

All you have to do to get a seat
on the bus is become pregnant.

"We are becoming the men we
wanted to marry." —Gloria Steinem

You might look as if you died
yesterday, but with a little rouge . . .

You can get drunk on less
liquor than a man can.

The average woman in the United
States lives seven more years
than the average man.

"A woman is always younger
than a man at equal years."
—Elizabeth Barrett Browning

Do you know any woman
who gets her deer or giant
swordfish stuffed?

These days, a lot of
men like to cook.

If not, there's the microwave.

"If a woman has to choose between catching a fly ball and saving an infant's life, she will choose to save the infant's life without even considering if there are men on base." —Dave Barry

We get a lot done in the middle of the night when we can't sleep.

Chick flicks.

There are an infinite number of red lipstick tones.

What We Know

We know what "season" we are.

❧

We know which eye droops.

❧

We know which foot is longer.

We know which calf is heavier.

☉

We know which breast is bigger.

☉

We know where to buy
Wacoal bras for less.

☉

We know what "a pinch
of salt" means.

We know when the recipe needs
more than a pinch of salt.

⟲

We know how many calories are in
every brand of cottage cheese.

⟲

We, unlike our husbands, know the
birthdays of our children.

⟲

We know how to braid
hair without looking.

We know the bride is two
months pregnant.

🌀

We know—though we might turn
out to be wrong—that the baby is
a boy by the way she is carrying.

🌀

We know Shelly had a nose job
even though she denies it.

🌀

We know which pants will
slenderize our thighs.

We know not to smoke
if we're on the Pill.

⟲

We know not to wear knee socks
before we head to the beach.
(They leave lines on our calves)

⟲

We know not to buy clothes
before our Junior Year Abroad in
Paris. We wait to buy them there.

We know not to use
spray-on deodorant
immediately after shaving.

🌀

We know the guy with the most
tattoos is not for us (although . .).

🌀

We know we should wait for July
to buy a new swimsuit on sale.

🌀

We know who the father
of our baby is.

We know which presidential
candidate is a better man.

🌀

We know all about washing our
hands after going to the bathroom.

🌀

We know not to eat
blueberry pie on a date.

🌀

We know what we wore
the night we met you.

We know what we ate at the
restaurant on our first date.

⑤

We know more than you think we
do about your old girlfriends.

⑤

We know how to knit
one and purl two.

We know how to throw away
the baby's breath in order to
make the arrangement from
the florist look expensive.

⑥

We know he's not right for you.

⑥

We know that even though he
says he'll call, he won't.

We can be "Miss," "Ms.," or
"Mrs." They can just be "Mr."

❀

"I have a brain and a uterus, and I
use both." —Pat Schroeder

❀

We rule charity work.

❀

Women can talk on the phone
like nobody's business.

We admit to our cosmetic surgery,
unlike some genders we know.

Adam's apples are kind of gross.

Men burp too much.

And that's not even the worst
sound they make (if you get
our drift).

Women have a higher body-fat percentage than men. No, wait! That's a terrible thing!

If you need an on-the-spot critique of your hairstyle, any woman can provide it.

The miracle of childbirth.

We mean, the miracle of blissful epidurals.

"Women are the architects of society." —Harriet Beecher Stowe

Better at applying self-tanner.

Better at telling you to
go clean your room.

Tiaras.

The gender that brought you
chocolate mint Girl Scout cookies.

Seven percent of men have
trouble seeing red and green.
Only 0.4 percent of women do.

We don't grab our own crotches.

Women's brains have a larger
corpus callosum than men's brains.
Doesn't that sound impressive?

What We'll Never Know

How to attach the
roof rack to the car.

⊙

How to get the car out of the
mud without calling AAA.

How to string the Christmas
lights on the roof.

❀

Which size bolt to use.

❀

Why they make so many
different kinds of screws (and
hence screwdrivers).

How far that plumber's "snake" should be wiggled down the toilet. (Although we can handle a plunger okay.)

⑤

Whether you're supposed to tip the gas station attendant.

⑤

When to get the oil checked.

Why guys get so mad
when we borrow their razor
to shave our legs.

6

Exactly what a prostate is.

6

What anyone finds appealing
about humongous muscles.

What's so great about *The Matrix*.

⟲

Why Armani costs so much less in
Milan than it does in Florence than
it does at the Mall of America.

⟲

How to convert to centigrade.

⟲

How to convert to kilos.

Where the WD-40 is.

❧

What WD-40 is.

❧

How certain people could have
been so wrong about WMD.

❧

Why you want to imagine me
as a "French maid."

Why you have to watch a cable replay of an entire baseball game you've already seen, live and in person.

⊙

Why you need a car that accelerates to 150 miles an hour when the speed limit is 55.

⊙

Why you're so passionate about naming your son after yourself (when you said you always hated your name).

The lyrics to the Metallica canon.

⑥

Which setting the printer
should be on: com1 or com2.

⑥

Why you have a crush
on Gina Gershon.

Why it's logical to wait until the gas tank is below empty before getting gas.

Why going to the airport on back roads instead of the highway is considered a shortcut even though it always takes longer that way.

Male pattern baldness?
No sirree, not for us.

They name ships after us.

And hurricanes too.

Don't need to wear ties to
convey our seriousness.

Can work on Wall Street and still
wear a Wonderbra.

Single pediatricians are
excellent candidates for
marriage and motherhood.

Women are more flexible than
men in every way, and we
won't bend on that.

We're so nice that we tell
one another we look good
even when we don't.

We're so nice we babysit
one another's kids.

Women make 85 percent
of all consumer-buying
decisions in America.

So good at buying gifts
that we get them for our
husbands to give to us.

It could be argued that we get
the better deal in polygamy.

"If you want something said,
ask a man. If you want
something done, ask a woman."
—Margaret Thatcher

It is the rare woman who has
to shave every day.

Even though she was single,
everyone wanted to date
Mary Tyler Moore.

That Joan of Arc could
really take the heat.

❀

They say women have great
intuition, and we have a
feeling that's true.

❀

"I Want a Girl Just Like the Girl
Who Married Dear Old Dad"

❀

"She's learned to say things with
her eyes that others waste time
putting into words." —Corey Ford

Quilting bees are more fun than
anything else you can do in a
grange hall.

Count on us to bring the coleslaw
to the church supper.

Far more men than women
have been indicted in white-
collar crime.

Every time we give birth,
our husbands are supposed
to buy us a present.

"Girls just want to have fun!"

There are still some girls who want
to grow up to be Miss America.

We can be rabbis.

We make terrific muses.

That Lucille Ball was a riot.

❀

"If truth is beauty, how come
nobody has their hair done in a
library?" —Lily Tomlin

What Men Think Women Do in the Ladies' Room

Have our toenails buffed by the automatic toenail-buffing machine that's standard in all ladies' rooms.

⊚

Take a nap on one of the foldout duvets—another ladies' room standard.

Help ourselves to the free buckets of beauty supplies and troughs of candy that are refilled every day.

6

Eat dinner, so when we return to the table we only want to pick at our salad.

6

Rendezvous with the cute trainer from the gym.

Shop.

☺

Watch reruns of soap operas.

☺

Take a quick steam.

☺

Practice kissing with inflatable
male dolls that we keep hidden
in our purses.

Tune in to the secret video machine that allows us to check up on our kids at school.

⊙

Eavesdrop on our dates, courtesy of the Ladies' Room Listening Tube.

⊙

Compare brands of toilet paper to see which is the softest.

Check the list of Bad Boyfriends
on the bulletin board.

⑤

Add items to the "Embarrassing
Things Our Husbands Do" list on
the same bulletin board.

⑤

Practice our secret handshakes.

⑤

Avoid the check.

What Women Really Do in the Ladies' Room

Talk about boys.

❀

Trade insider tips.

❀

Trade tips about how to remove wine stains.

Trade homework answers.

⑤

Draw anatomically correct
diagrams.

⑤

Enact cosmetic and coiffure
interventions.

⑤

Argue about whether we'd
rather date Antonio Banderas
or George Clooney.

Return our food to a
more biodegradable state.

⑥

Tarot card readings.

⑥

Study Kabbalah.

⑥

Prepare for our book clubs.

Participate in focus
groups about hairspray.

(6)

Give ourselves "fingertip facelifts"
in the mirror.

(6)

Complain about how few
stalls there are.

(6)

Avoid the check.

Branwell Brontë sank into drinking and drug use, whereas his sisters Charlotte and Emily became mainstays of the high school English curriculum.

Women's perfume is so much classier than men's cologne.

Our wallets have change compartments.

Our bicycles don't have that
annoying horizontal bar.

Our underwear is sexier
than their underwear.

Likewise, our shoes.

Where would the self-help book
business be without us?

Not to mention novels—we read
many more than men do.

"Women deserve to have more
than twelve years between the
ages of twenty-eight and forty."
—James Thurber

Mary Poppins was
supercalifragilisticexpialidocious.

Aunt Sallie Shadd, a freed slave,
perfected ice cream as we
know it today.

❀

Is there anything cuter than a
four-year-old girl in a tutu?

❀

Yes. A ballet recital full of them.

We've inspired some of
the greatest poems.

❀

And love letters.

❀

And show tunes.

❀

And excuses.

We're so imaginative we believe
the dry cleaner shrank our pants,
rather than face the fact that
we've put on three pounds.

Our own salad dressing:
Green Goddess

Some of the Seven Sisters
colleges are so inclusive they
accept boys.

There were seven dwarfs
but only one Snow White.

We can use our long hair
to cover our faces.

We can take our husband's
last name. Or not.

Our driving isn't as
bad as they say.

And, despite what they say, we
can be generous tippers.

Nobody else would put the
photos in the family album.

❀

Very few of us leap onto
the table when there's a
mouse in the house.

❀

Can you believe we made pureed
organic dill chicken baby food
for the baby when he was
eight months old?

We know what we'll wear
to a birthday party five
weeks from now.

It's much more acceptable for
women to wear men's clothes
than vice versa.

Okay, guys can wear earrings
nowadays, but we still look
better in them.

Why We Can't Get Rid of Anything in Our Closets

Might fit into it again someday.

Planning to have the waist let out.

Need it for "fat days."

🌀

Back when we were sophomores,
Todd said he liked this sweater.

🌀

It would be too embarrassing to
get rid of it while the sales tags
are still attached, and taking them
off would take too much time.

I hate that color, but the saleslady
said it was very flattering.

⊚

Might want to go skiing
again sometime.

⊚

Any year now, it's going to
come back into style.

Those old shoes are too dusty
to look at, let alone put into
a bag for Goodwill.

🌀

It's ugly, but it's a *classic*.

🌀

Quincy Jones complimented it
when I met him on the elevator.

Exhibit A in my lawsuit
against the dry cleaner.

⑥

Is it right to give the homeless
cruise wear with a missing belt?

⑥

Never wore it, never will, but too
expensive to throw out.

Tux of old boyfriend—saved
in case I need excuse
for getting in touch.

☉

Keeps my other
white shirts company.

☉

What if I suddenly learn the
violin and am asked to give a
recital at Carnegie Hall?

How can I ditch the dress I wore
to my brother's first wedding?

⑥

Someday I'll hem this.

⑥

Ahead of its time.

⑥

Vintage-to-be.

Mom gave it to me, and she might
check to see if it's still in here.

⑥

If I just iron it, it'll look great.

⑥

Can wear it when we paint
the summer house.

⑥

Saving it for Halloween.

"Show me a woman who doesn't feel guilty, and I'll show you a man." —Erica Jong

❀

Sex and the City was a very popular show.

❀

We believe in therapy.

❀

And couples counseling.

And talking about the relationship.

But don't criticize us.

"I have seen too much not to know that the impression of a woman may be more valuable than the conclusion of an analytical reasoner." —Arthur Conan Doyle

"Women and cats will do as they please, and men and dogs should relax and get used to the idea." —Robert A. Heinlein

Females learn foreign languages
more easily than males.

A female bird's drab coloration
protects her from predators.

Less likely to have beer bellies.

Hot flashes are useful
in the winter.

There's always a little spare
change at the bottom of a purse.

Chanel No. 5.

At proms, boys don't get
to wear corsages.

When a woman swears, it
has more impact.

"Bitch" isn't quite the
dis that it once was.

Men aren't allowed to care about
what kind of decorative soap goes
in the guest bathroom.

Clear nail polish is good for
stopping a run in panty hose.

And nail polish remover is
good for lots of things.

Can't drive in a convertible without
ample hair accessories.

"A woman can say more in a sigh
than a man can say in a sermon."
—Arnold Haultain

Any decade now, women will
truly be treated as equals.

Less tendency to marry models
thirty years our junior.

A woman is likely to have a
spare tissue on hand.

We can tell what kind of day our
kids had just from the way they
plunk their backpacks down on the
kitchen counter.

"It goes without saying that you
should never have more children
than you have car windows."
—Erma Bombeck

You never hear anyone say
"My dad has the best recipe
for meatloaf."

When a woman parallel-parks,
well, it's a big deal.

"You were once wild here.
Don't let them tame you."
—Isadora Duncan

What We Call You-Know-What

At high tide.

Aunt Flo is visiting.

Can't go swimming.

🌀

Closed for maintenance.

🌀

The curse.

🌀

The dot.

Falling off the log.

⑥

Falling off the roof.

⑥

Grandma.

⑥

Having mechanical difficulties.

⑥

I'm not pregnant.

It.

☺

Time of the month.

☺

Mother Nature's staying
in my hotel.

☺

Old faithful.

Thanks to Title IX, girls now
get just as many knee
injuries as boys do.

Being a woman means never
having to swat your own hornet.

Say what you will, Lady
Macbeth was very persuasive.

After all this time, it's still the
guy's job to take out the trash.

Although we are physically capable
of lifting heavy boxes, there always
seems to be some man around who
will relieve us of the task.

We aren't embarrassed about
buying "hygiene products."

Men aren't as likely to receive
flowers on Valentine's Day.

At a wedding, the bride
always gets way more
attention than the groom.

"Horses sweat. Men perspire.
Women glow."

At the all-women Stephens
College, you can board your horse.

Women go to church more than
men—so women are more likely to
get into heaven.

Men are rarely referred to
as "my better half."

"Sugar and spice and everything nice" trumps "Snakes and snails and puppy-dog tails."

"Never eat more than you can lift." –Miss Piggy

Men can't wear turbans on bad-hair days.

Our stretch marks are worn with pride.

If you want to show off your
legs, wear a tennis skirt.

Often it's the candidate's wife
who is responsible for his victory.

You can always find a
flattering way to wear black.

We remember where the cookie
decorations are stashed.

"A woman must have money and a room of her own." —Virginia Woolf

We still do more than our share of the housework, as all the latest studies remind us.

Show us a *man* who ever knew a folk remedy.

We look better wearing ruffles and gold chains.

(And we look way cool in tuxedos.)

Our deodorants smell so pretty!

We're the ones who
housebreak the puppies.

We control the diet-cola market.

We're not required to barbecue.

We Know What Goes With . . .

A gray pinstripe
pant suit–a white T-shirt

&

Khaki trousers–a white T-shirt

A flouncy summer
skirt–a white T–shirt

⑥

A black chiffon wrap
skirt–a white T–shirt

⑥

A Hawaiian printed
maillot–a white T–shirt

A pearl choker—a white T-shirt

🌀

Blue jeans and sneakers
—a white T-shirt

🌀

A white T-shirt—a white T-shirt

🌀

A glass of red wine—a black T-shirt

Any horrible thing we do
we can blame on PMS.

Women's laps are more
comfortable to sit on.

"It has been women who have
breathed gentleness and care into
the hard progress of mankind."
—Queen Elizabeth II

Hillary Clinton.

We bond over bad—blind date tales.

Amazingly courageous when it
comes to protecting our young.

Only a woman would buy a
spurious antique out of pity
for the shop owner.

Women know better than men
which tie goes with which shirt.

A woman will throw away her
husband's ratty old sweatshirts
without any compunction.

It's not as embarrassing to
overhear a woman singing
along with her iPod.

Women have a better instinct
about how to bag items in
the supermarket.

Girls are less likely to be
autistic than boys.

At camp, girls' cabins pass
inspection more often than
boys' cabins.

Today's teenage girls aren't
ashamed to bare their tummies
even if they're a little pudgy.

We can spend the whole day with
our best friend, then come home
and spend the whole evening
talking to her on the phone.

"The two women exchanged the kind of glance women use if no knife is handy." —Ellery Queen

It's said that girls make the best pearl divers.

We're no longer expected to ride sidesaddle.

Angels are traditionally depicted as female.

Men would never dare to
collect ceramic owls.

A bad female dancer is better
than a bad male dancer.

If Jack hadn't fallen down and
broken his crown, Jill would still
be up on the hill.

Little Women far
outsold *Little Men*.

"Ginger Rogers did everything
Fred Astaire did, and she did it
backward and in high heels."
—Faith Whittlesey

No one gives a husband
an anniversary ring.

In nineteenth-century
fiction, widows were sexy.

Say what you like, Becky
Sharpe had a lot of guts.

Men look a little weird
playing the harp.

You can count on us to put
in a new roll of toilet paper.

And to leave the seat down.

Strategies for Surviving the End-of-Season Shoe Sale

Try not to be a size eight.

☉

Get invited to the private pre-sale.

Arrive early.

ⓖ

Make derisive remarks to the sales-
people about the other "animals."

ⓖ

Stow shoes you haven't decided
on under your chair.

ⓖ

For the shoes you know you
want, wear them around the
store to imprint them, as
it were.

Use your elbows.

⑥

Bribe a salesman.

⑥

Tell fellow customers that the
shoes they're considering
make ankles look fat.

⑥

Hire a bodyguard.

Tips for Women Eating Alone While Traveling

Reread menu for subtext.

❍

Rename your lipstick.

Pretend you are the real J. Crew
and come up with new and
amusing ways to describe colors.

⑥

Limit yourself to one
alcoholic drink.

⑥

Make up a new budget.

⑥

Revise new budget.

Pretend to be talking
on your cell phone.

⑥

For God's sake, don't
catch anyone's eye.

⑥

Don't order lobster or any other
food you have to wrestle with.

Bury yourself in a magazine
(preferably *The Economist*,
not *Us*).

☺

Resolve to order room
service in the future.

The name "Juliet" has held up a lot better than the name "Romeo."

"Can you imagine a world without men? No crime and lots of happy fat women." —Nicole Hollander

All shampoos work pretty much the same, but we cling to the touching belief that there's a perfect one out there.

In all the *good* countries, we have
the right to vote.

Taking hormones gets us through
menopause without a hitch.
Oh, wait—

The bride gets to carry a bouquet.
The groom doesn't.

We're not obligated to know how
to change a tire, but men are.

In coed touch football, an
aggressive female player scares
the pants off the guys.

❀

Nowadays, no one comes into
your house and gives the furniture
the "white glove treatment" to
see how well you've dusted.

❀

In a crowded elevator, people
will more readily make room for a
woman than for a man.

Only a woman can fool herself
into thinking that half a cup of
yogurt is dinner.

❁

(And, later that night, fool
herself into thinking that a
twelve-ounce bag of chocolate
chips has no calories because
she's standing up to eat it.)

❁

When there's a scary sound
downstairs at night, it's the
husband's job to check it out.

No one expects you to work
on your tan anymore.

❀

Dame Edna likes women so
much she became one.

❀

If the only magazines at the
dentist are issues of *Good
Housekeeping*, it's okay for us to
read them. Guys just have to sit
there with nothing to read.

Our higher percentage of body
fat may save us when we're lost
in the Arctic.

Little boys don't get to wear
ponytails and barrettes unless
they have *very* liberal moms.

Most of the "mini mags" at
the checkout counter are
aimed toward women.

No one looks at a woman
funny if she's filing her nails.

❀

Chastity belts are a
thing of the past.

A woman can tell you how
to get rid of that stain.

❀

"There's another button just like
the one you lost in the button
jar on my bureau."

How to Make School Pickup Fun and Profitable

Think up excuses for getting out of going to the next PTA meeting.

⑥

Use your Blackberry to order groceries.

Tailgate Ethan's mother.

☺

Privatize the school-bus system.

☺

Circulate a petition
demanding that third-
graders have less homework.

Find out whether the tenth-grade
Honors English teacher is having
an affair with the principal.

⑥

Spread rumors about a certain
mother in the seventh grade.
(You know who.)

⑥

Schedule various medical
checkups for your kids from
now until graduation.

Always carry intimidating tomes
and make sure the cover is visible.

⑥

Take notes for the tell-all book
you plan to write about your
daughter's school.

⑥

Interrogate little Lilah Chapman on
where her mother really is.

⑥

Our Mutual Friend on tape =
thirty-seven hours.

We buy mother-in-law cards on
Mother's Day and let our husbands
pretend they picked them out.

"Because I am a mother, I am
capable of being shocked—as I
never was when I was not one."
—Margaret Atwood

"We are not amused."
—Queen Victoria

When we get that tone in our
voice, you'd better listen up.

Real live women rarely hit men over
the head with a rolling pin.

Or get tied up on railroad tracks.

"Okay, you can have chocolate
milk just this once."

❀

Once mastered, the art of
playing jacks never leaves you.

❀

We remember to water the plants.

We have an innate sense of what
to say in a receiving line.

"I can bring home the bacon,
fry it up in a pan, and never
let you forget you're a man."
—Vintage TV commercial

We say we don't want fries with
that, then we eat all your fries.

"The supply of good women far exceeds that of the men who deserve them." —Robert Graves

A woman knows all the "alternative" methods for hemming a skirt on short notice: tape, pins, glue, etc.

"Of course I remember how to make a Chinese jump rope!"

"Of course I remember how to make a gum-wrapper chain!"

❀

When a movie heroine takes off her glasses and shakes out her hair, she automatically becomes beautiful.

❀

"An actress can only play a woman. I'm an actor, I can play anything." —Whoopi Goldberg

Julia Child's *Mastering the Art of French Cooking* is the best book in its field.

❀

We're good at identifying flowers.

❀

We don't have to wear skating skirts on the rink these days.

Don't tell us about passive
aggression. We practically
invented it. Likewise,
suffering martyrdom.

❀

"We are the hero of our own
story." —Mary McCarthy

Our Top Argument-
Winning Lines

"I'm not going to talk about
it anymore."

"A mother always knows."

"There's no way I can
make you understand."

@

"I'm not asking you;
I'm telling you."

@

"If Isabelle jumped off the bridge,
would you jump off the bridge?"

@

"I *knew* you'd say that."

"I'm the mommy, that's why."

𝒢

"And this to the woman who bore your children!"

𝒢

"You'll thank me someday."

𝒢

"I'm only doing this for your own good."

"That's exactly what a
man *would* think."

◎

"Do I look like I have
three hands?"

◎

"I just have a bad
feeling about it."

◎

"Because."

We get extra brownie points
for mowing the lawn.

The wonderful day when
we finally get to pick out
our own clothes.

Some men still can't pick out
their own clothes.

"When I am an old woman, I shall wear purple." —Jenny Joseph

It's okay for us to like wine that's a little too sweet.

Maya Lin designed the Vietnam Veterans Memorial in Washington, D.C., when she was only twenty-one.

Nothing wrong with us that a
Frappuccino can't fix.

Face it—our faults are just
cuter than guys' faults.

"I hate women, because they
always know where things are."
—Voltaire

Catherine Blaikley, a Colonial Williamsburg midwife, delivered more than three thousand babies.

Women have been able to vote in Mississippi since 1984, when the state finally ratified the Nineteenth Amendment.

"I've been a woman for a little over fifty years and have gotten over my initial astonishment."
—Nadia Boulanger

There is no one more assiduous
than a teenage female seeking
out split ends.

As King Lear said of Cordelia,
"Her voice was ever soft, gentle,
and low—an excellent thing in
women." (Wait! What the hell was
he talking about?)

Every mother's daughter would
love to visit the American Girl Doll
Store—even without a child in tow.

Our long, strong fingernails
can easily slice open packages,
make origami folds, and pull
ticks off dogs.

Oh, how adorable we look
wearing a man's button-down
shirt as our pj's.

We will cheerfully read *The
Runaway Bunny* aloud forty-nine
times in a row.

Surely rocking chairs were
invented for women.

"Flight attendant" will never sound
as natural as "stewardess."

"Once a woman is made man's
equal, she becomes his superior."
—Margaret Thatcher

We keep the depilatory
industry alive.

❀

To say nothing of the
romance genre.

❀

"Women speak two languages—
one of which is verbal."
—William Shakespeare

❀

Without looking it up, we know
that eight ounces equals one cup.

Height isn't a status thing with
women the way it is for men.

"Age cannot wither her, nor
custom stale her infinite variety."
—Shakespeare in *Anthony
and Cleopatra*

We can make a cross-country
trip holding the map upside down
the whole way.

Women don't snore as
often or as loudly as men.

American Women's Firsts

1587: Virginia Dare was the first person born in America to English parents.

❀

1650: Anne Bradstreet was the first published American woman writer.

1777: Mary Katherine Goddard became the first printer to offer copies of the Declaration of Independence that included the signers' names.

☺

1795: Anne Parrish founded the House of Industry, the nation's first charitable organization for women.

1809: Mary Kies became the first American woman to receive a patent—for a method of weaving straw with silk.

☺

1849: Elizabeth Blackwell received her M.D. from the Medical Institution of Geneva, New York, becoming the nation's first woman doctor.

1864: Rebecca Lee Crumpler, graduating from the New England Female Medical College, became the first black woman to receive an M.D.

⑥

1879: Belva Ann Lockwood was the first woman admitted to practice before the U.S. Supreme Court.

1879: Mary Baker Eddy was the first woman to found a major religion: Christian Science.

🌀

1885: Sarah E. Goode became the first African-American woman to receive a patent, for a bed that folded up into a cabinet.

1896: Alice Guy Blaché, the first American woman film director, shot *The Cabbage Fairy*, her first of more than three hundred films.

☙

1901: Annie Edson Taylor, a schoolteacher from Michigan, was the first person to go over Niagara Falls in a barrel.

1921: Edith Wharton was the first
woman to win a Pulitzer
Prize for fiction.

1922: Rebecca Felton became the
first woman senator (though she
served for only two days).

1926: Gertrude Ederle was the first woman to swim the English Channel.

☺

1932: Amelia Earhart was the first woman to fly solo across the Atlantic.

☺

1934: Lettie Pate Whitehead became the first woman in the nation to serve as director of a major corporation (the Coca-Cola Company).

1946: Edith Houghton became the first woman hired as a major-league baseball scout.

⑥

1953: Jerrie Cobb was the first woman to undergo astronaut testing.

1960: Oveta Culp Hobby became the first woman to serve as Secretary of Health, Education, and Welfare. (She was also the first woman to be awarded the U.S. Army Distinguished Service Medal.)

1965: Patsy Takemoto Mink was the first Asian-American woman elected to Congress, serving for over twenty-four years.

1967: Althea Gibson was the first
African–American tennis player to
win a singles title at Wimbledon.

1972: Sally Jean Priesand became
the nation's first woman rabbi;
Juanita Kreps became the first
woman director of the New York
Stock Exchange (and later, the
first woman to be appointed
secretary of commerce).

1975: Elizabeth Ann Seton was canonized, making her the first American-born saint.

⑥

1981: Sandra Day O'Connor was the first female justice appointed to the Supreme Court.

1985: Wilma Mankiller was elected
first woman chief of the
Cherokee Nation of Oklahoma.

1990: Dr. Antona Novello was
sworn in as U.S. surgeon
general, becoming the first
woman, and the first Hispanic,
to hold that position.

1992: Carol Moseley Braun was the first African-American woman elected to the U.S. Senate.

1993: Toni Morrison was the first African-American woman to win the Nobel Prize for Literature.

1997: Madeleine Albright was sworn in as secretary of state—the first woman to hold the job.

🌀

1999: Nancy Ruth Mace graduated as the first female cadet from the Citadel.

🌀

2001: Condoleezza Rice became the first woman to serve as national security adviser.

"Give me a dozen such heartbreaks, if that would help me lose a couple of pounds." –Colette

Drag queens are so jealous of us!

Nuns are scarier than monks.

Unlike men, we know that
"vanilla" and "vanilla extract"
are the same thing.

❀

We're not ashamed to talk
baby talk to dogs.

❀

A new mom will discuss her
episiotomy with total strangers.

What male would ever buy
books with titles like *Our
Bodies, Ourselves?*

Men look silly in aprons.

We are good at putting up
pictures by affixing little rings of
Scotch tape on the back.

We even remember our
godchildren's birthdays.

(As well as the dog's birthday.)

(And we give the dog a
little party too.)

Maybe the house wouldn't win
any cleanliness prizes.

If reminded, we will send
a postcard to nieces and
nephews at camp.

"Women are never landlocked—
they're always mere minutes away
from the briny deep of tears."
—Mignon McLaughlin

We cried real tears over *The Bridges of Madison County.*

In the back of our big encyclopedia, there's a pressed flower from the time we took that walk with Tom in high school.

We don't talk to fundamentalists when they come to our door, but we do buy candy and wrapping paper from kids raising money for the sophomore class.

❀

We always have a secret stash of babysitters.

Sometimes we even give one of
their names to a trusted friend.

❀

Women are allowed to say that
clothes are cute. Men aren't.

❀

In fact, we have exclusive
rights to "cute."

One thing we'll never have to
worry about: being too macho.

It's more fun to watch the women
gymnasts during the Olympics,
even if the men do have more
"explosive power."

Little kids and country-music
stars refer to us as "ladies."

Doris "Granny D" Haddock walked across the country at age eighty-nine to promote finance reform.

Everyone remembers that Natalie Wood played Maria in *West Side Story*. Nobody remembers who played Tony.

"There's a great woman behind every idiot." —John Lennon

Ask a man what an opal looks
like, and he won't know what
you're talking about.

❀

Boys don't get to have
Sweet Sixteen parties.

❀

Eggs are rarer than sperm.

Not-So-Rare Allergies of the Female

Too much Paco Rabanne.

⊙

Hairy ears.

Men with ungroomed
toes in sandals.

❻

Men with toenail polish.

❻

Men who tell you what
everything costs.

Noise.

(6)

The Three Stooges.

(6)

Hidden food in the crack
of the seat cushion.

Someone who uses the phrase "the whole nine yards" every seventeen seconds.

⊚

Working "Harvard" into every sentence.

⊚

The *Lethal Weapon* movie and its sequels.

Men who never ask you a single
question about yourself.

ⓖ

Men who go to a party
without you and then bring
home no gossip.

ⓖ

Men who go manic with
a TV remote.

Men who keep pennies in jars.

6

Men who keep their dirty laundry
on the floor of the closet.

6

Men who set their watches
five minutes fast.

Men who drive through yellow
lights when we try to follow them.

6

Men who leave empty milk
cartons in the refrigerator.

6

Men who borrow your reading
glasses and can't remember
where they put them.

Men who don't tell you before
you need the car for carpool that
there's no gas left in the tank.

☺

Men who threaten to blow
up the world.

Who was more sparkly—
Cher or Sonny?

❀

Who was more fascinating—
Cleopatra or Antony?

❀

Who was more glamorous—
Marilyn Monroe or Arthur Miller?

Women float more easily than men.

The Taj Mahal was built
for a woman.

Our stiletto heels are
good lawn-aerators.

A woman doesn't usually have
to wear a truss.

❀

"Being a woman is of special
interest only to aspiring male
transsexuals. To actual women,
it is simply a good excuse not to
play football." —Fran Lebowitz

❀

Stroller handles are way too
short for most men.

Back in the olden days, women
didn't have to fight duels.

Or go to war.

Or pump their own gas.

Our skin is petal-soft.

Our eyes are like stars.

❀

Our teeth are like pearls.

❀

Women don't have to wear nightgowns anymore—T-shirts and boxers are fine.

Flowered bathing caps are history.

"We hold these truths to be
self-evident, that all men and
women are created equal."
—Elizabeth Cady Stanton

The female worker bees are the
ones that make the honey. Drones
just sit around waiting to mate.

Cows are the ones that give milk.
Bulls just stand around waiting to
mate (and gore people).

"Heaven will protect the
working girl." —Edgar Smith

We can describe the difference
between mauve and lilac.

We're better than men
at folding clothes.

❀

If it was called Father Nature,
trees would be done in chrome.

❀

"Whatever women do they must
do twice as well as men to be
thought half as good. Luckily,
this is not difficult."
—Charlotte Whitton

We may not be great at it, but
we can thread a needle.

❀

We can fake the foxtrot
better than a guy.

They're really closing in on good
razors for women.

❁

We're so tenderhearted!

❁

Face it. You can't get
along without us.

Attributes All Playboy Playmates Have in Common

They dislike "pushy people."

❻

They like long walks on the beach.

They dislike smokers.

🌀

They like saline implants.

🌀

They dislike put-downs and
show-offs.

🌀

They appreciate honesty and
skinny-dipping in the ocean.

They like sitting in front
of the fireplace.

⟲

They like snuggling.

⟲

They love Hugh Hefner.

They like French manicures.

⑥

They like Brazilian waxes.

⑥

They dislike nine-to-five jobs.

"Life on the planet is born of woman." —Adrienne Rich

Barbies have such tiny little feet!

The slogan "If I have only one life to live, let me live it as a blonde" was coined by a woman.

When we're in a group, we always
seem to get our cycles into sync.

Jane Austen, Jane Austen,
Jane Austen.

It's okay for us to collect
porcelain figurines.

Likewise, porcelain thimbles.

We don't press down too
hard on our crayons.

✿

There is no substitute for
a woman (except maybe a
Stouffer's frozen dinner).

✿

Without women's magazines,
the entire Jell-O empire
would collapse.

"A woman needs a man like
a fish needs a bicycle."
—Irina Dunn

❀

We can be trusted around
a bottle of bleach.

❀

We don't pretend to know
how to fix the dishwasher
and end up breaking it.

There will never ever be a male
Miss America.

"One is not born a woman,
one becomes one."
—Simone de Beauvoir

Magazines are using more
plus-size models.

We always put our hands behind a candle flame when blowing it out.

We have opinions about whom comic-strip characters should marry.

Key-lime juice for pies is now readily available in bottles.

We're no longer called on to
trim our own bonnets.

"We poets would die of
loneliness but for women."
—William Butler Yeats

In a church choir, women altos
can usually pinch-hit for tenors.

Wow! Now there's surgery
to reshape your middle-aged
belly button!

❀

When we're backing into a
parking space and we hear a
funny little scraping noise,
we bravely keep going.

❀

We could just number our children
in the order they appear, but we
go to all the trouble of picking
out nice names for them.

We can show you how to make
a dandelion chain.

Try and find a man who owns a
pair of pinking shears!

"I've given my memoirs far more
thought than any of my marriages.
You can't divorce a book."
—Gloria Swanson

Our voices don't change in the
croaky way that boys' voices do.

New Pageant Titles

Miss Malleable.

❍

Miss Saving Up for Law School.

❍

Miss Behaved.

Miss Doesn't Look Like a
Member of Mensa.

6

Miss Doesn't Look Like a Member
of Mensa but Is.

6

Miss Never Read a Book.

6

Miss Nothing Moves.

Miss Saving Up for Gender
Reassignment Surgery.

⑥

Miss I Have a Talent that Nobody
Considers a Talent.

⑥

Miss Ultra-Conservative Member of
Christian Right Who Looks Like Las
Vegas Working Girl.

⑥

Miss Gets God into
Every Sentence.

How many female figure-skaters
can you name? How many
male ones?

"I married beneath me—all
women do." —Nancy Astor

Of course you can borrow
our emery board.

"Somewhere the gods
have made for you the
woman who understands."
—Everard Jack Appleton

"Cautious, careful people, always casting about to preserve their reputation and social standing, never can bring about a reform. Those who are really in earnest must be willing to be anything or nothing in the world's estimation."
—Susan B. Anthony

"I myself have never been able to find out precisely what feminism is. I only know that people call me a feminist whenever I express sentiments that differentiate me from a doormat or a prostitute."
—Rebecca West

Women keep a stash of birthday
and get-well cards on hand,
just in case.

We never outgrow our
love of stickers.

Men don't get to wear a bathing
suit with a skirt.

Atalanta beat all those
guys in that race.

Luna brand protein bars
are just for women!

The Billie Jean King versus
Bobby Riggs tennis match was
so damn satisfying.

"Does feminist mean large,
unpleasant person who'll shout
at you, or someone who believes
women are human beings? To me
it's the latter, so I sign up."
—Margaret Atwood

"The history of men's opposition
to women's emancipation is more
interesting, perhaps, than the
story of that emancipation itself."
—Virginia Woolf

Mini, Micro Mini, Maxi skirts.

Mini, Micro Mini, Maxi pads.

You never know when that old
nurse costume will come in handy.

Bangs, no bangs, perms, body
waves, highlights, lowlights—your
hair need never bore you.

"Ah, women. They make the
highs higher and the lows more
frequent." —Anonymous

Everyone looks svelte in
a pencil skirt.

It's okay to circle your *i* dots.
It's not okay for a guy to do that.

What We're Thinking About When We're in the Stirrups

Why didn't I wax my legs?

𝕲

I feel nothing.

Is it possible that this burns calories?

G

Should I get my tummy tucked?

G

You'd think at these prices they could afford 100 percent cotton robes.

I really need a massage.

⑥

I really need a Valium.

⑥

I wonder who Madonna's
gynecologist is.

⑥

I forgot to leave money for the
cleaning lady.

How hard can this be? I should have gone to medical school.

⑥

Dr. Lyon looks worried. What did she find?

⑥

I hope she doesn't ask me when I had my last period because I have no idea.

Was I supposed to pick
up Rachel?

⑥

Who colors Dr. Lyon's hair?

⑥

Closed for renovations.

Marching in Washington with a
pregnant belly makes you look
even more sincere.

❀

Moving to the head of a long,
long ladies' room line when
you are pregnant.

❀

We get diamond engagement rings.

A two-hour pedicure.

With paraffin.

We have two cable networks, just
for us: Oxygen and We.

Kegels work.

By contrast, we're the nice judge
on *American Idol*.

"The gate of the subtle and profound female is the root of Heaven and Earth." —Lao-tzu

Our hairdressers love us.

One day they'll invent drive-through Botox and collagen procedures.

By the way, boys don't have Botox parties.

"The silliest woman can manage
a man, but it needs a very clever
woman to manage a fool!"
—Rudyard Kipling

In a pinch, a fresh Tampax can
double as a Handi-Wipe.

You can jot down a telephone
number with lip liner.

Funny how a new bra can
lift your spirits.

"A successful woman preacher was once asked, 'What special obstacles have you met as a woman in the ministry?' 'Not one,' she answered, 'except the lack of a minister's wife.'"
—Anna Garlin Spencer

You never have enough black shoes.

They expect us to go to spas.

You know what? I'd prefer to spend my fortieth birthday with my women friends.

A dolman sleeve is very forgiving.

"Women and elephants never forget an injury." —Saki

A new issue of *Vogue*.

"I have found it impossible
to carry the heavy burden of
responsibility and to discharge my
duties as king as I would wish to
do without the help and support
of the woman I love." —King
Edward VIII, while abdicating

Even your husband
understands that you simply
need more earrings.

It's biologically predestined
that we care about our skin,
our nails, our figures . . .

And that they are better than
Sandi's skin, nails, and figure.

We get extra credit for
being good drivers.

"Sometimes I wonder if men and
women really suit each other.
Perhaps they should live next door
and just visit now and then."
—Katharine Hepburn

We know our way around a
feather duster and a pastry bag.

We get the cute, frilly aprons.
Men have to wear canvas
barbecue aprons printed
with stupid jokes.

What We Keep in
Our Briefcases

Bottle of water and nuts in
case of national emergency.

⑥

Rebecca's pacifier.

Three pens that do not work.

❧

Dog chew for Beanie.

❧

One glove.

❧

Two identical lipsticks.

Business card from
odious man at party.

⑥

Paint swatches.

⑥

Lots of lint.

⑥

Unwrapped hard candy with lint.

The all-male production of *The Women* never has quite the same effect.

You can be a girls' girl or a guys' girl.

You can even be one of the guys.

But you can't be "just good friends" with the guys.

"We only want that which is given naturally to all peoples of the world, to be masters of our own fate, only of our fate, not of others, and in cooperation and friendship with others."
—Golda Meir

The ability to elongate yourself by wearing the same color top, pants, and heels.

Nobody makes guesses about your sexuality if you happen to love show tunes.

Sephora is a good way to
spend a few hours.

Even a chubby woman can look
sleek in a riding habit.

It is more likely that Wayne
Newton will dedicate a song to
you than to your boyfriend.

One day in the future,
your insurance will pay for
breast implants.

A handsome gynecologist.

✿

"I am a woman above
everything else."
—Jacqueline Kennedy Onassis

✿

It is easier for women to get jobs
as lottery-number callers.

✿

"Women are like tricks by sleight
of hand, which, to admire, we
should not understand."
—William Congreve

You don't have to apologize for loving *Friends* reruns.

Tennis skirts make tennis more fun (at least when we go into town afterward).

Some guys think they *have* to bring you flowers every time they see you.

"Well-behaved women rarely make history." —Laurel Thatcher Ulrich

1,003 Great Things About Being a Woman

Sam has a crush on you!
Sam has a crush on you!

Ladies' Night beers just cost one dollar.

You can never have enough pashminas.

Samplers made long ago by twelve-year-old girls now sell for thousands of dollars.

These days, no one minds if your handbag and shoes don't match.

"Women would rather be right than reasonable." —Ogden Nash

The beach boy realizes you need help putting up your umbrella.

You finally found the perfect red T-shirt!

"I am neither a man nor a woman but an author." —Charlotte Brontë

Women's Math

How many pairs of black pants we need = Are you familiar with the concept of infinity?

⑥

How many pairs of black shoes we need = One more pair than we can afford.

How much we would pay to find that perfect pinky-brown-nude lipstick = We'd be willing to trade our collection of pinky-brown-nude lipsticks.

6

How much they would have to pay you to wear the tube top you wore to the senior picnic to your twenty-fifth reunion = Seventy-five thousand dollars.

How much to make out with
Paul Acorn again = One hundred
twenty-five thousand dollars.

⊙

How much to wear the tube top,
make out with Paul Acorn, and let
him tell the football team what you
look like at forty-three = Have you
ever heard of "imaginary numbers"?

⊙

The number of decibels we just
yelled = We weren't yelling, we were
just e-nun-ci-a-ting clear-ly.

How many inches around our
waists = Two inches fewer than
the tightest we can pull the
measuring tape.

⑥

How much we weigh = Three
pounds more than our highest
weight *ever*.

⑥

How many teaspoons of baking
powder in our recipe for
chocolate cake = You mean
our secret recipe? Oh,
about seventeen.

How far it is to the second floor of the house = Too far while we're cooking, so could one of you kids please go up and get Mommy a sweater?

6

How many hours of sleep we got last night while waiting for you to come home = Not one wink.

How many times you need to call your child at college = Twice a day, first semester freshman year. Once a day by second semester. First semester sophomore year: twice a week. Second semester sophomore: once a week. Junior Year: once a week. Senior Year first semester: twice a week. Second semester: twice a day.

⑥

How fast we were driving = Officer, I'm sorry for crying but I'm pregnant and my husband just left me and did anyone ever tell you how cute you look in a uniform?

We always know where there is a
spare needle and thread.

"There's wisdom in women, of
more than they have known."
–Rupert Brooke

It's no longer necessary to wear
hose to church or synagogue
on a muggy, hot day.

It's okay to let someone
else turn over the mattresses.

Like Vanessa Williams, we can
rehabilitate our images and
even one day become
corporate spokeswomen.

A bubble-gum-pink leather agenda
looks spiffy in your purse.

And is admired by
everyone who sees it.

248

Ditto your purple
patent-leather wallet.

❀

Meeting friends for coffee
and realizing you've spent three
hours together.

❀

Jared has two mommies and so
does Megan and so does Lucy.

❀

"A little more matriarchy is
what the world needs, and I
know it. Period. Paragraph."
—Dorothy Thompson

So many new novels these days, written just for us.

We can never have enough perfume.

We can never have enough perfume.

Most of us don't waste brain space on *The Workings of the Automobile.*

Wearing jewelry doesn't necessarily make you look frivolous.

You can get away with
whimsical socks . . .

And the occasional strange hat.

You can look dumb but be very smart.

Edith Wharton: great writer, great
hostess, and she was rich.

Words We'd Like to See

Penwomanship.

❀

Herstology.

❀

Antiherstomine.

❀

Womenstruate.

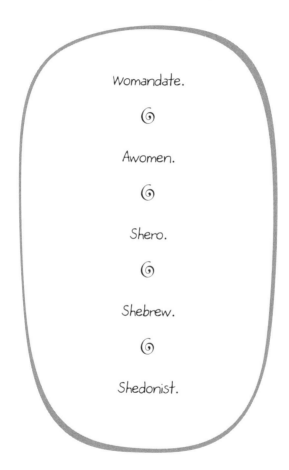

Womandate.

⑤

Awomen.

⑤

Shero.

⑤

Shebrew.

⑤

Shedonist.

Womandible.

🌀

The Isle of Woman.

🌀

Womanx cats.

🌀

Heralayas.

🌀

Womantlepiece.

🌀

Womanagement.

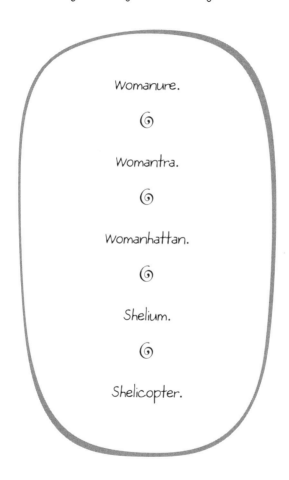

Womanure.

⑤

Womantra.

⑤

Womanhattan.

⑤

Shelium.

⑤

Shelicopter.

Womanifesto.

☺

Womanic, womaniacal.

☺

Fu Womanchu.

☺

Chef Girlardee.

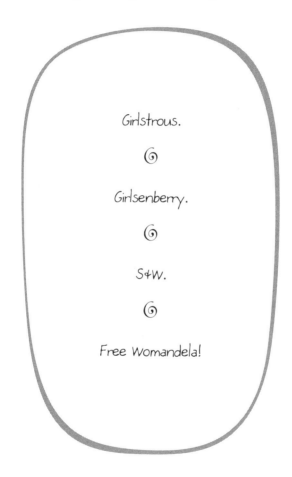

Girlstrous.

Girlsenberry.

S&W.

Free Womandela!

"Men are like fine wine. They start out as grapes, and it's up to women to stomp the crap out of them until they turn into something acceptable to have dinner with." —Dave Barry

There are more and more women film directors now.

No one teases us for wearing pink.

Some panty girdles go all the way down to the knees.

Wrist corsages: so
passé they're hip.

"Toughness doesn't have to
come in a pinstripe suit."
—Dianne Feinstein

Over-the-knee boots are
sexy and don't make us
look like a Musketeer.

Eligible to fight in the U.S. military.

More women contestants on
While You Were Out on the
Learning Channel.

We never go shopping without
thinking about buying something
for our loved ones.

Rose Kennedy was still hat-shopping
after her one-hundredth birthday.

"So much has been said and
sung of beautiful young girls,
why don't somebody wake up to
the beauty of old women?"
—Harriet Beecher Stowe

Pamela Digby Churchill Heyward
Harriman had the best death:
while swimming in the pool at the
Hotel Ritz in Paris.

No one, not even Elle Macpherson
looks good in a fanny pack.

"There is no female mind. The brain is not an organ of sex. As well speak of a female liver."
–Charlotte Perkins Gilman

Sports bras.

You still have your hair.

Though you look good in that wig.

And that straw hat with fake
hair attached to it.

There's a firehouse around the
corner from your house.

And three of the
firemen are single.

It's okay to order the clutch bag
you saw in *InStyle* magazine.

Female affirmation chain e-mails.

Our eyelashes can be long,
longer, longest!

You can now get your
eyelashes permed.

One of These Days We'll Get Around To . . .

Vacuuming under the bed.

☙

Learning not to blame
ourselves for everything.

☙

Losing eight pounds.

Passing the Equal
Rights Amendment.

⑥

Cleaning out the attic.

⑥

Getting a new diaphragm.

⑥

Polishing the silver.

⑥

Becoming more assertive.

Recycling all our old magazines.

☺

Learning Italian.

☺

Having a baby.

☺

Learning how to
program our TiVo.

☺

Solving the nation's
child-care problem.

Sending Virginia and Phil a
wedding present.

⑥

Breaking up with Howard.

⑥

Finding our marriage license/social
security card/birth certificate.

⑥

Writing back to our
sophomore year roommate
who sells insurance.

Buying a new shower curtain.

⊚

Filling in the baby book of our
third child (age eleven).

⊚

Seeing the world.

⊚

Trying a Brazilian wax.

⊚

Backing up computer files.

Checking to see if our ex's profile
is on match.com.

☙

Reading *War and Peace*.

☙

Making dinner from scratch.

☙

Helping women who suffer
under oppressive regimes.

Redeeming that ancient gift
certificate at Elizabeth Arden.

☺

Finding the perfect mascara.

☺

Self-acceptance.

West Point is no longer a dream.

If you win an election, you
become a role model for
younger women.

"When people ask me why I
am running as a woman, I
always answer, 'What choice do
I have?'" —Pat Schroeder

Personal shopping is now a real
career (to a small segment of the
population, anyway).

272

"Oh, I know her too!
Small world!"

❁

Nail salons on every block.

❁

It's fun to realize you
gained weight *there*.

❁

"Show me someone not full of
herself and I'll show you a hungry
person" —Nikki Giovanni

Grosgrain ribbons are back.

So is Lily Pulitzer.

Let's face it: no one expects
you to be too decisive.

You *need* a wardrobe of sunglasses.

Shelf bras that are sewn
into tank tops: what genius!

Bike shorts are slimming.

Acting girlish at your age.

Acting girlish at any age.

Acting girlish as a senior citizen.

"I now know all the people worth knowing in America, and I find no intellect comparable to my own."
—Margaret Fuller

Without ever having been there, we know our way around every Target, Wal-Mart, Kohl's, and Kmart.

Just try to find a guy who's brave enough to go through labor.

On average, women live
longer than men.

❀

According to the census, 71
percent of teachers in the
United States are women.

❀

Society no longer considers us
"strumpets" for putting on a
little makeup.

Great Things About Lesbian Weddings

Everyone's on the bride's side.

⑥

A couple that can really
wear matching outfits.

You can count on someone(s) to
write the wedding announcement.

♉

You can give them "hers and hers"
lingerie as wedding presents.

♉

Or gift certificates at
the makeup counter.

No more struggling with uncooperative cummerbunds or pesky bow ties.

⑥

Diamonds for both spouses.

⑥

No raucous stag party.

Less likely to have reception
ruined by drunken usher
gatoring to "Soul Man."

⟲

More likely to have reception
ruined by drunken bridesmaid
doing Tracy Chapman karaoke.

⟲

More likely to resemble a
mixer at Smith College.

Something for Massachusetts and
Ontario to brag about.

6

Honeymoon at Canyon Ranch Spa.

Boys get ear infections more
frequently than girls.

The song goes "Can *she* bake
a cherry pie . . ."

Even though smiling gives us
crow's feet, we keep doing it.

Patti Smith is still rockin'.

Men get no points
for being curvaceous.

"There is no animal more invincible
than a woman, nor fire either, nor
any wildcat so ruthless."
—Aristophanes

It's been awhile since a woman
was tried for being a witch. At
least in the United States.

"Winter, spring, summer, or fall,
All you have to do is call . . ."
—Carole King

We finally have our own religion—
Wicca. (Too bad it's kinda dopey.)

Female officers are addressed as
"Sir" on *Star Trek*.

For quite a long time, we actually
thought we had a chance to marry
Paul McCartney.

Women are more likely than men
to take out library cards.

"When I marry him, I'll
change all that."

Hemlines can be anywhere we
want them nowadays.

They now make teeny hairbrushes
to fit inside our teeny purses.

Being your best friend's
daughter's godmother.

❁

Some cell phones are so small
they don't even make unsightly
bulges in our pockets.

❁

The power of an innocent
sixteen-year-old girl.

Or younger. Think Lolita.

Women can be famous
just for being stylish.

That milk ad just reminded me:
time for a lip wax!

Body hair is no longer
nature's imperative.

Ditto curly hair.

Ditto straight hair.

Ditto brown hair.

Ditto gray hair.

Ditto a broad behind.

Ditto small breasts.

Ditto large breasts.

We've Come a Long Way, Baby

Nail wraps.

❻

Eyelash perms.

❻

www.DailyCandy.com

Shoemakers who can change the
heel height of expensive shoes.

☺

Internet supermarkets.

☺

Chopped salads.

☺

Cell phones with cameras.

LASIK surgery.

⑥

Cellulite-decreasing panty-hose.

⑥

Over-the-counter teeth-
whitening systems.

⑥

Sunblock.

Whenever Angelina Jolie gets a
new tattoo, it's a photo op.

"Is it too much to ask that women
be spared the daily struggle for
superhuman beauty in order to
offer it to the caresses of a
subhumanly ugly mate?"
—Germaine Greer

Your old wrap skirt still fits.

They're bringing back espadrilles.

And Bermuda bags.

Your mother may think of massages as a luxury, but for our generation they are a necessity.

The amazing way our bodies accommodate our growing babies.

The politeness of people who
assume we won't discuss our age.

❀

"When men reach their sixties and
retire, they go to pieces. Women
go right on cooking." —Gail Sheehy

❀

No one expects us to curtsy
anymore—except, perhaps,
Queen Elizabeth.

❀

That dream you had last night
about Senator Joe Biden was
incredibly erotic.

Older men think you
look really good.

Personal maintenance can take up a
whole morning, until you're supposed
to meet your friends for lunch.

"I find a woman's point of view
much grander and finer than a
man's." —Katharine Hepburn

Receiving flowers is still a treat.

It's amazing what a
difference bangs can make.

The new generation of panty
girdles are so light and breathable.

Spray-on stockings. (They have
silk in them. Honest.)

People appreciate our
pretty penmanship.

The song and show are
called "*Mama Mia*."

No matter how old we get, we
still remember the camp cheer.

"Somewhere out in this audience
may even be someone who will one
day follow in my footsteps and
preside over the White House as
the president's spouse. I wish him
well!" —Barbara Bush

We will always need a
string of pearls.

What's with boys and guns?

Two words: hostess gifts.

We don't mind if a man holds
a door open for us.

For some reason, we're always the ones who hold doors for women with strollers.

There are always women online to e-mail bad news and warnings.

You can be renowned for your cleaning skills.

If plastic surgery scares you, you
can always get a facial.

If a facial scares you, you can
always buy a new top.

"I would rather trust a woman's
instinct than a man's reason."
—Stanley Baldwin

How to Break Up with Your Hairdresser

My new cult believes that
tinting hair taints one's soul.

⊚

My son the doctor quit medical
school to become a hairdresser.

My moon is not compatible
with your moon.

⑥

My new boyfriend loves really,
really long hair and asked me
never to cut it. Ever.

⑥

Maybe when I come back from
the Peace Corps in Eritrea,
I can call you?

I've been drafted by the
New Jersey Nets and
am shaving my head.

☉

I've become so religious, I am
leaving the world of vanity.
Good-bye hair!

Another beauty salon is
actually paying me to have
my hair highlighted there.

☉

I'm under house arrest.

I've just developed an
allergy to everything.

⊙

Suddenly, I have a scissors phobia.

⊙

It's not you; it's me.

Retail therapy is
unexpectedly effective.

No one is surprised if you
overpack for the weekend.

We have enough fat in our bodies
for the surgeon to inject a little
into our cheeks when they sag.

We're so conscientious, no one
expects we're actually playing
Solitaire/Tetris/Word Whomp
at the office.

"Man works from sun to setting
sun, but woman's work is never
done." —Anonymous

The gentle tapping sound of toe
shoes in a ballet performance.

Katherine Graham was the
backbone of the *Washington Post*.

Everyone likes Louise
Nevelson's sculptures.

Way less involved in drug
trafficking than men.

We look sexy in geeky
reading glasses.

Toe cleavage is sexy.

Most husbands will let their
wives have the bigger closet.

Or more space in their closet.

Edamame are particularly
healthy for us.

Erma Bombeck was really funny.

We no longer have to wear
corsets (unless we are
Gaultier models).

We know that a kiss
can cure a boo-boo.

Christina Crawford would never
have sold as many books called
Daddy Dearest.

We're never embarrassed
about wearing pink.

We've even gotten
men to wear pink.

We're not embarrassed to
sign our letters "Love."

If you fall in the volleyball
tournament, we sincerely mean it
when we ask, "Are you okay?"

We don't like to go to
bed with wet hair.

We don't throw clean
socks in the hamper.

Do the words Tolerant, Gentle,
Artistic, Stylish, and Willowy
mean something to you?

Men just don't get it
the way women do.